This
Book
Belongs
To _

An
ALICE
IN
BIBLELAND®
Storybook

The
STORY
Of
JOSHUA

Written by Alice Joyce Davidson
Designed by Victoria Marshall

Text copyright © 1989 by Alice Joyce Davidson
Art copyright © 1989 by The C.R. Gibson Company
Published by The C.R. Gibson Company
Norwalk, Connecticut 06856
Printed in the United States of America

The C.R. Gibson Company, Norwalk, Connecticut 06856

A little girl named Alice
Had some favorite things to do.
She liked to read, to sing, to dance
And play on her kazoo.

One day she took a storybook
And read a Bible story
About a man named Joshua
And how God gave him glory.

As Alice read, the airmail bird
Circled overhead.
He dropped a note right by her feet,
And this is what it said:

"Reading is the magic key
To take you where you want to be."

The Bible storybook she read
Became a giant screen.
Alice walked through it to Bibleland,
And came upon this scene.

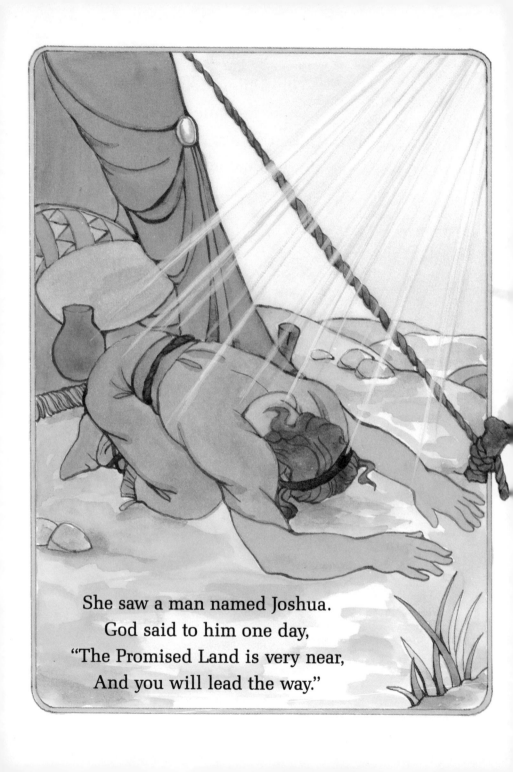

She saw a man named Joshua.
God said to him one day,
"The Promised Land is very near,
And you will lead the way."

Joshua told the Israelites,
"God gave me a command.
I'm to lead you forward,
To Canaan, your Promised Land.

"I'm sure that God will help us,
And when three days have passed,
We'll cross the Jordan River
And we'll be home at last."

But on the Jordan's other side
Was a wall both tall and wide
With the well-protected city
Called Jericho inside.

Two spies were picked by Joshua
To go that very night,
To find out if the Canaanites
Were ready for a fight.

They crossed the Jordan River,
Then climbed to Jericho.
The spies looked for a hiding place,
But found no place to go.

The mighty king of Jericho
Had heard that spies were there.
He sent his well-trained soldiers
Who went searching everywhere.

The soldiers went from house to house
To find the spies that night;
But a brave woman named Rahab,
Hid them out of sight.

Rahab told the Israelites,
"I know that you're our foe,
But God will give you victory
When you take Jericho.

"The soldiers here are frightened,
And know they'll lose the fight.
We know God protects your people
With His power and His might.

"And when you conquer Jericho,
Remember, I hid you.
Promise that you'll save my life
And all my family, too."

Rahab helped the spies escape.
When Joshua heard their tale,
He knew they'd conquer Jericho—
God would not let them fail.

Then Joshua told his people,
"Tomorrow right at dawn
We'll cross the Jordan River,
And then we'll travel on."

Early in the morning
As the sun rose in the sky,
The Israelites' priests led the way,
Their golden Ark held high.

The Ten Commandments were inside
The golden box that day.
When the priests walked in the river,
The waters rolled away.

The Israelites all followed
Across the river bed.
They were on their way to Canaan
And to Jericho ahead.

As they approached the giant wall,
The entrance to their land,
Joshua saw an angel
With a sword held in his hand.

"I'm the captain of God's army,
I am under His command.
Listen and God will tell you
How to win the Promised Land."

Later Joshua gathered
Every woman, every man
Every single Israelite,
And told them of God's plan.

The walls surrounding Jericho
Were tall and strong and wide.
It would take a miracle
For them to get inside.

Horns loudly blew!
They marched around
The walls day after day,
And God was with the Israelites
To help in every way.

On the seventh day, said Joshua,
"Today's the day we win!
Shout and play your trumpets.
Let's raise a mighty din!"

They marched around for seven times,
There came a thunderous sound.
The mighty walls of Jericho
Came crashing to the ground.

The Israelites rushed to the city.
They quickly won the fight.
Then Joshua remembered
A promise made one night.

He saved Rahab and her family.
Then they joined the band.
And just as God had told them,
They had their Promised Land.

The time had come for Alice
To leave this Bible scene.
She walked away from Bibleland
And came back through her screen.

Alice thought, "I learned a lot
Today in Bibleland.
God gave Joshua the faith
To take a mighty stand.

"And God is with each one of us
Who follows in His way.
He'll guide us and He'll lead us
And He'll bless us day by day!"